WHO WORKS IN MY NEIGHBORHOOD
THE
VETERINARIAN
Jared Siemens
LIGHTBOX
openlightbox.com

LIGHTBOX

Go to
www.openlightbox.com
and enter this book's
unique code.

ACCESS CODE

LBXN8399

Lightbox is an all-inclusive digital solution for the teaching and learning of curriculum topics in an original, groundbreaking way. Lightbox is based on National Curriculum Standards.

OPTIMIZED FOR

- ✓ **TABLETS**
- ✓ **WHITEBOARDS**
- ✓ **COMPUTERS**
- ✓ **AND MUCH MORE!**

STANDARD FEATURES OF LIGHTBOX

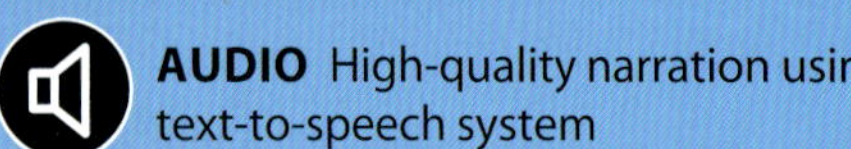

AUDIO High-quality narration using text-to-speech system

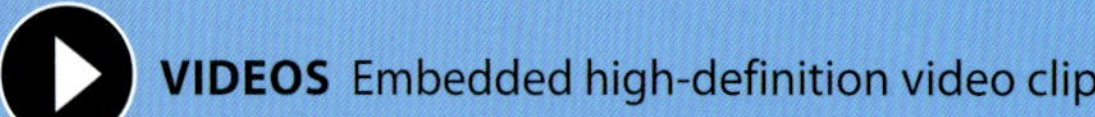

VIDEOS Embedded high-definition video clips

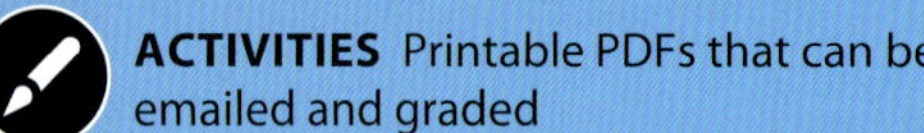

ACTIVITIES Printable PDFs that can be emailed and graded

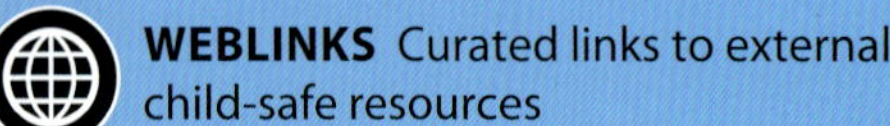

WEBLINKS Curated links to external, child-safe resources

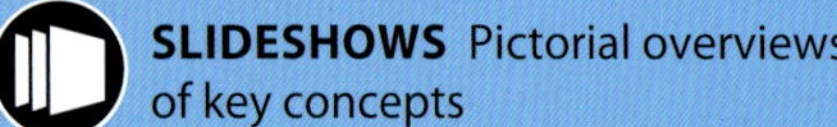

SLIDESHOWS Pictorial overviews of key concepts

INTERACTIVE MAPS Interactive maps and aerial satellite imagery

QUIZZES Ten multiple choice questions that are automatically graded and emailed for teacher assessment

KEY WORDS Matching key concepts to their definitions

VIDEOS

WEBLINKS

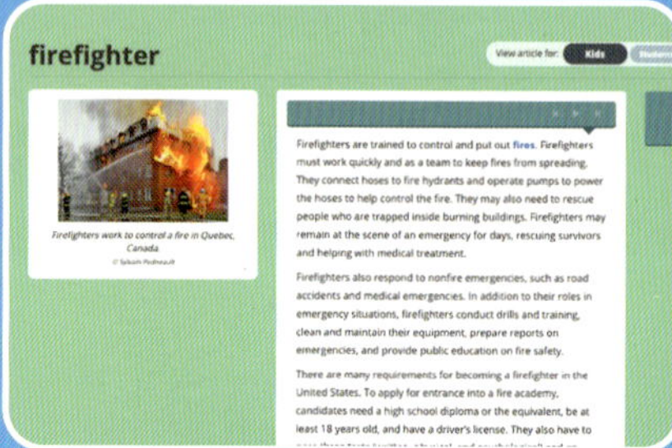

SLIDESHOWS

QUIZZES

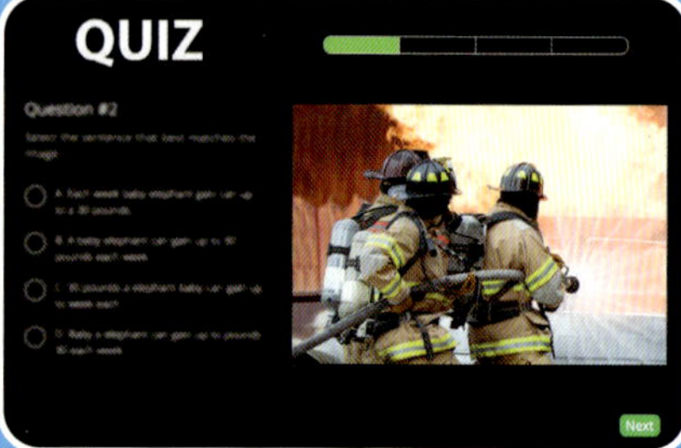

WHO WORKS IN MY NEIGHBORHOOD

THE VETERINARIAN

Contents

The veterinarian is a person in my neighborhood.

6

A veterinarian works in an animal hospital.

The **Patterson Dog and Cat Hospital** in Michigan is one of the **oldest** animal hospitals in the **United States**.

A veterinarian is an animal doctor.

About **90 million dogs** are kept as **pets** in the **United States**.

The veterinarian makes sure my pet is healthy at checkups.

The veterinarian uses many tools to find out what is wrong with my pet.

About **4.5 million** Americans have at least one pet **snake**.

The veterinarian puts a bandage on my pet's leg to help it heal.

The veterinarian knows what medicine my pet needs to get well.

Veterinarians help all kinds of animals.

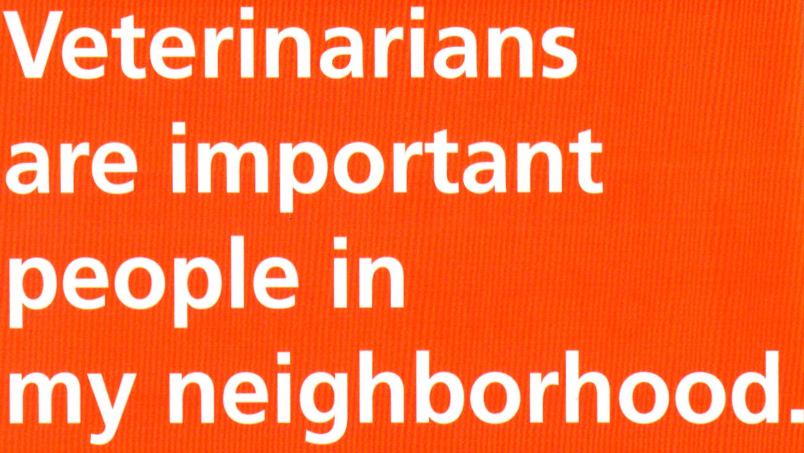

Veterinarians are important people in my neighborhood.

There are about **71,000** veterinarians in the United States.

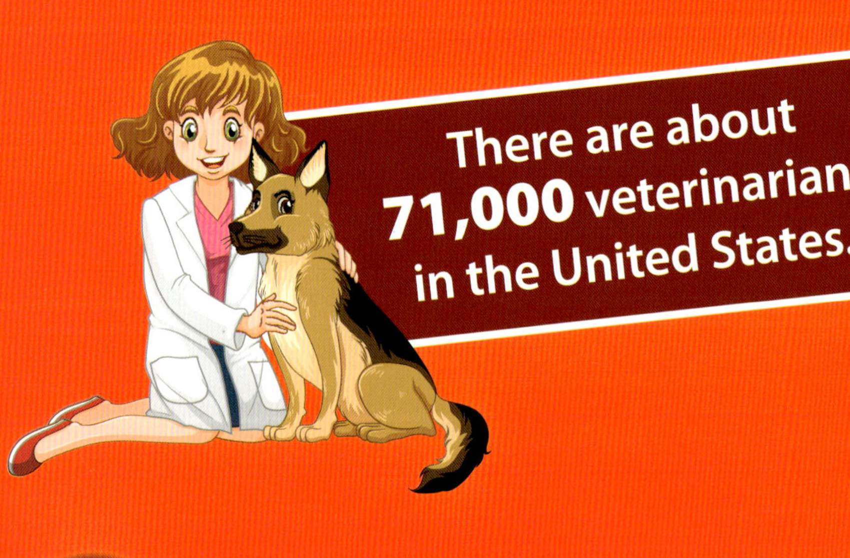

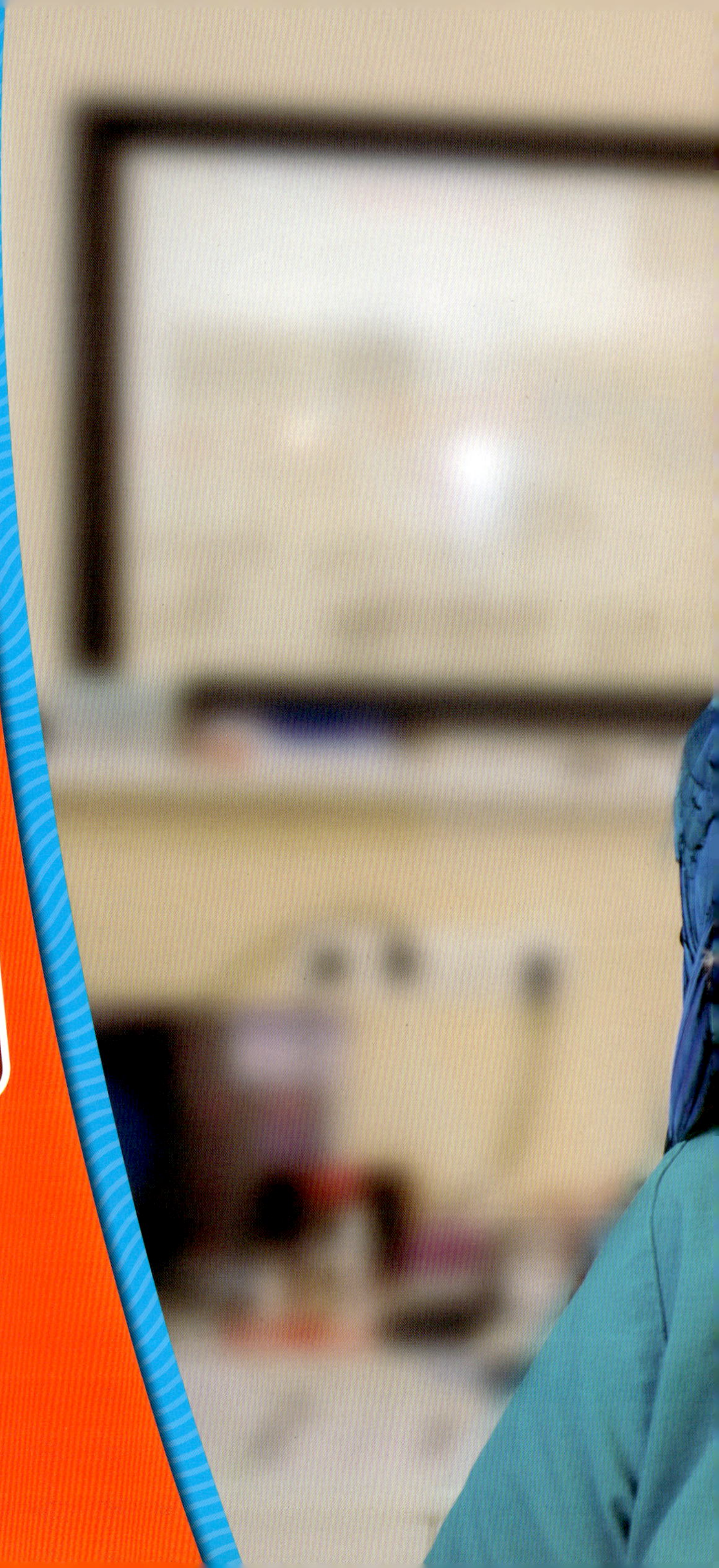

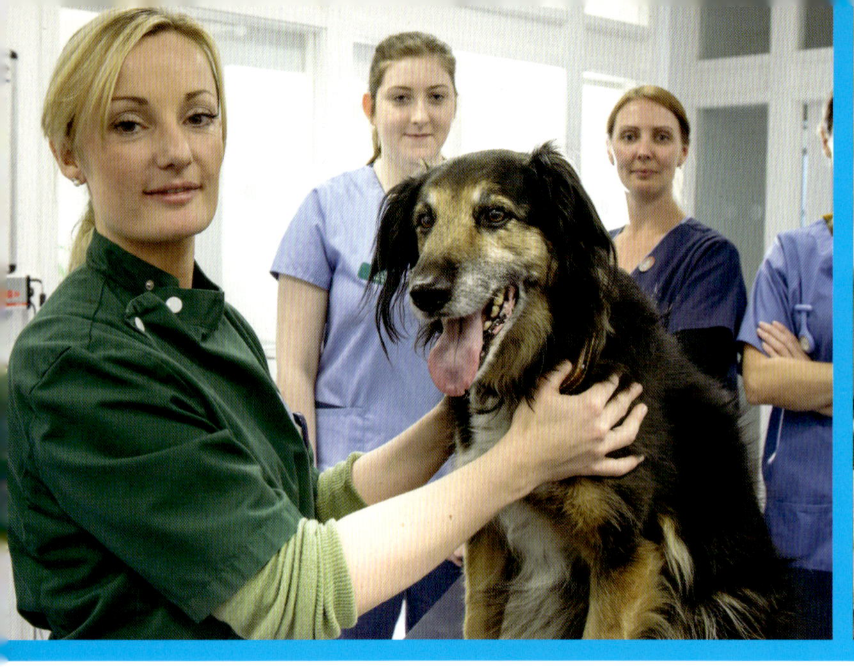

See what you have learned about the veterinarian.

Describe what you see in each of the pictures.

KEY WORDS

Research has shown that as much as 65 percent of all written material published in English is made up of 300 words. These 300 words cannot be taught using pictures or learned by sounding them out. They must be recognized by sight. This book contains 38 common sight words to help young readers improve their reading fluency and comprehension. This book also teaches young readers several important content words, such as proper nouns. These words are paired with pictures to aid in learning and improve understanding.

Page	Sight Words First Appearance
4	a, in, is, my, the
7	an, and, animal, of, one, states, works
8	about, are, as
10	at, makes
13	Americans, have, many, out, to, uses, what, with
14	help, it, on, puts
16	get, knows, needs, well
19	all, kinds
20	important, people, there

Page	Content Words First Appearance
4	neighborhood, person, veterinarian
7	animal hospital, Michigan, Patterson Dog and Cat Hospital, United States
8	doctor, dogs, pets
10	checkups, healthy
13	snake, tools, wrong
14	bandage, leg
16	medicine

Published by Smartbook Media Inc.
350 5th Avenue, 59th Floor, New York, NY 10118
Website: www.openlightbox.com

Library of Congress Control Number: 2020934518

ISBN 978-1-5105-5361-3 (hardcover)
ISBN 978-1-5105-5362-0 (multi-user eBook)

Printed in Guangzhou, China
1 2 3 4 5 6 7 8 9 0 24 23 22 21 20

042020
110819

Project Coordinator: Ryan Smith
Designer: Ana María Vidal

Every reasonable effort has been made to trace ownership and to obtain permission to reprint copyright material. The publisher would be pleased to have any errors or omissions brought to its attention so that they may be corrected in subsequent printings.

The publisher acknowledges Getty Images, iStock, and Shutterstock as the primary image suppliers for this title.